Pellet Stove and Hot Tub Repair Simplified

TIM JOHNSON

Copyright © 2023 Tim Johnson

All rights reserved.

ISBN:
ISBN-13: 9798387413810

DEDICATION

This little booklet is dedicated to the do-it-yourself crowd, those with little money that have to make it stretch and those held hostage by manufactures that refuse to sell parts outside of authorized repair facilities or are unable to supply parts because of "shortages". Exorcism of these computerized controls becomes necessary when parts become unavailable. Fortunately, somewhat generic control parts are available to help create your retrofit solutions.

CONTENTS

	Foreword	i
1	My tub Story	1
2	Methods Of Spa Control	3
3	Analog And Hybrid Controls	4
4	Spa And Furnace Controllers	6
5	Thermal Wrap Pumps And Lighting	8
6	Pellet Stoves And Smokers	10
7	Switches And Rheostat Controls	11
8	Burning Cordwood Or Construction Waste	14
9	Timer Controls	15
10	Plugged Auger Tubes	17
11	Pellet Stove Timers And Parts	19
12	Disclaimer	23

FOREWORD

This particular foray down the path of literary marginalism started because of my experiences with a certain hot tub, one of their suppliers and, my first pellet stove, an Avalon, gave me plenty of lessons in timer circuit controls and their applications. Lessons learned helped me to help others with their hot tub and pellet stove issues. Hopefully this little guide will help you. Whether it be a hot tub or pellet stove that you've owned for years or a cheap or free appliance that you want to resurrect. Perhaps you need a tub for therapy purposes or just want to add one to your home relaxation or entertainment plan. Whether it's a pellet stove you've had for years or one you want to set up as an alternate heat source for home, shop or garage. I won't go into the diagnosis of these items' specific problems, there are lots of youtube and other internet guides to help you there. Those guides will get you to the point where you know a computer has failed. This guide is for bypassing those computer controls to get your appliance up and running again when those computerized parts are just unaffordable or unavailable. THIS GUIDE ALSO ASSUMES THAT YOU HAVE THE ELECTRICAL BACKGROUND TO SAFELY WORK INSIDE THESE APPLIANCES. Craigslist, Facebook, newspapers and bulletin boards are good places to find items that the previous owner has given up on. Many times you can get them free. Pellet stoves show up at the dump all the time. Smaller dumps usually have an employee that will keep you apprised of new arrivals and help you out. Be sure to pay these people for their help. My first Hot tub was a rescue tub and after replacing a few freeze broken fittings, bypassing the broken filter assembly and replacing the thermostat, I had a hot tub for an investment of less than $100. Just in time too because that's when I really screwed my back up at work the first time and the tub proved invaluable for getting me back to work. My first pellet stove was an old timer type, the rheostat had "dead" spots in it and the momentary switch for setting the 900 second timer wasn't working at all anymore. Even the lamp was burned out. A bunch of research, $25 in parts off ebay and it lived again. Well, there was an issue inside the auger tube as it had sat exposed to the elements full of pellets. I'll go into how I cleaned that mess out in the section on pellet stoves below......

1 MY TUB STORY

Way back in the mid to late 2000's, my wife and I purchased a hot tub we saw demonstrated at the fair in Bishop California. Living in Nye County Nevada, they decided to send it to New York City instead. At considerable expense on their part I might add. So, over a month after we bought it, the darned thing finally arrived on the truck. We got all the cool toys for it and it was a dream come true. For about a month. Then it became a bad dream, perhaps even a Night Mare, that black horse that plagues us when everything is just going too well. The pump failed. No problem, just get the company to send us a new pump and we would be back in action? Right? Wrong. They wont send us a part, they DEMAND that we send the module containing the pump and electronics to them at our expense for warranty consideration. No, I don't have time for this horse shit nonsense when I am more than qualified to repair it myself. Sell me a new pump then and I'll just fix your POS myself. Wrong! They wouldn't sell even the smallest part of their base hot tub unit outside of their repair facilities and certainly not to someone that thinks they can fix a hot tub. So, their fancy shamancy little pump is a flooded electric motor. The water from the hot tub cools it, it is also the only heat source for the hot tub. It is how the water is heated, by the waste heat produced by the inefficiency of the motor. Kind of brilliant design. Except that the slightest particle of anything suspended in the water will lock the motor up or damage the pump portion. Both of which had happened. I traced the failure back to particles shed by the chlorine tablet device thingy (very technical, right?). At this point, I contact the manufacturer of the pump itself and they refuse to sell me a new pump. Why? Because of the predatory nature of their agreement with the tub manufacturer. Because they know it's going into a one of this manufactures tubs, they can't even sell me one of their similarly configured pumps. "Fine, not a problem". That's what I told them. I then went on to explain that I was going to open a facebook account that's sole purpose would be to warn people about these tubs and their pumps and their brand name as the pump manufacturer would appear prominently. They sent me a new pump configured to fit the my tub at no cost and asked that I send the old one back for failure analysis. I refused to send it back as I figured I might need the parts to keep my pump running until I engineered a replacement for their crappy design. It turned out that a few months later, I would need those parts to repair another failure. This time I think it was the stator coil that failed. Regardless, within a year of receiving the tub, I was on my third repair of the pump and motor and I started researching in earnest for a solution. I found a pump made by Balboa with a 1.5 HP motor and a snap on plastic heat "coil" that would allow the hot tub to both cool the motor and use this heat supplied by the motor losses to heat the hot tub. Cost at that time was about $339 as I remember. Evidently the problem was so wide spread that a new design sprung up to address it? You have to butcher the styrofoam of the pedestal assembly somewhat to get the larger pump assembly into it, but it worked well for years until an electrical screwup sent 240 to the electronics and fried the controls several years later. Then the tub manufacturer wouldn't directly sell me a new logic board or control box and wanted it sent to a service center. Price of the board was in the $1200 range plus diagnosis and installation. Again, my attitude and refusal to be dictated to kicked in and I decided that they could keep their fancy shamancy electronics that drive up the cost of hot tubs and maintenance of hot tubs and just go back to analog. What is analog? It's what has worked for so many years, reliably, before the digital age smacked us on the head and drove the cost up on everything and made things less reliable and harder for the end user to service. Thermostatic switches. For a hot tub, you need two. One to regulate the temperature and another as a reset-able high limit switch, in line with the first one in case it fails. This interrupts the power and keeps your machine from running until it boils, melts down or cooks someone to death, or alive. Don't get me wrong, I love my tub but the way they run the company? Not so much. Hopefully the issue with the pump design was eventually addressed and no longer an issue.

2 METHODS OF SPA CONTROL

Today, I see a few ways to bypass and replace the spa controls that are so failure prone, with components that are relatively easy to work with, inexpensive and long lasting. First: Analog controls. Second: A hybrid mixture of analog and solid state switching devices. Third: An inexpensive aftermarket spa or even a furnace controller with solid state relay control of the motor. Four: A wireless monitor and controller option, which could also be used with a solid state relay to make the electronics even more reliable. I will speak on the application and advantages of each option and give suppliers and part numbers needed. Fifth: I will also go into a more efficient heating method and the possibilities of dual pumps for larger hot tubs requiring more water flow. Many hot tubs contain flow switches and filters and some of these controls and accessories can be safely deleted by redesigning the system. A cleanable and fully reusable suction filter can be added inside the hot tub itself that simply slips over the pump inlet, this allows the difficult to access filter to simply be deleted. Many hot tubs have separate electrical panels with GFCI breakers and when retrofitting, an inline GFCI can be installed if it is desired to simplify the system or rust and corrosion have rendered other systems inoperable or too expensive to fix. In that case, the old boxes can become junction boxes for the new wiring.

3 ANALOG AND HYBRID CONTROLS

In the early days of the mass production of home hot tubs and spas, the electronic controls simply did not exist. Pumps and heaters were controlled by thermostats. Lights and compressors were controlled by toggle switches. It was a simpler time and also a less expensive time when it came to repairs. Larger systems that took more amps than could be directly switched by the thermostat used relays. Although, these days, I would not even think of using a mechanical relay. The solid state relays are inexpensive and very reliable. So, for the basic analog system, you will need a high limit switch, a thermostatic switch and a solid state relay or two, depending on pump size and heater amperage. A couple toggle switches might be needed to control lights, compressor or pump override. Say you want the pump to run while the heat isn't turned on? Add another switch and separate solid state relay to control that function. The simplest would consist of a thermostatic switch and a pump that uses the heat generated by the motor to heat the water. This system would lack any over heat safety though and you would have to monitor the temperature quite closely with your floating thermometer to make sure you aren't going to cook once you step into the hot water. Adding a high limit switch could save a life. Your choice. Your thermostatic switches use a capillary tube and a bulb that inserts into a dry well in the piping of your pump. This allows the electrical component to monitor temperatures of the water. Most systems use 1/4" or 5/16" diameter bulbs. The size is important. I have even seen 3/8" but only a couple of those. The tube must be long enough to reach from the switch location to the control box area. They come in various lengths to allow this. They generally slide into the well and are retained by a blob of RTV silicone applied over the top. Don't glue them into the hole itself or you will play hell getting them back out when tearing down for service or replacement. To get the old wire type sensor or previously used capillary style, simply use a screw driver to dig out the silicone around the top of the sensor and the old part SHOULD slide right out. Most thermostats made for hot tubs are adjustable between 80f and 106f degrees and the length can be 6" to 60". They start at less than $40 at hottubspasource.com They are for 120 VAC, if you have a 230 VAC pump or heater, use a double pole relay to control the pump, heater or both. Flow or pressure switches are placed in line with the control voltage of the thermostat to make sure heat does not come on without pump flow. The reset-able high limit switches are similarly configured, place them in line with the thermostat in case it fails, that way the power to the pump and or heater will be interrupted. High limit switches are set for 107f degrees and they cost about the same as the thermostat. If you need a solid state relay, the easiest place to find them is on eBay. Find one that comes with a heat sink and has the primary and secondary voltages in the range you need and able to handle the amps needed with a comfortable margin. They also are available with one side being DC, so be aware of what you are buying because those will flame out spectacularly when used with AC. I use them regularly with furnace controls in the mining industry and have used the wrong ones before. That is the problem with a certain green oven that are supplied with both AC and DC controls, complacency means mistakes will be made. Vevor now makes a hot tub and spa heater. The thermostat is built in and has a line cord to wire into your junction box. 1.5" hose connections and 3000 watts. All that for $125.

4 SPA AND FURNACE CONTROLLERS

Furnace controllers can operate a hot tub quite nicely as long as the desired temperature is within their design specifications. The ones I am referring to are industrial controls that are used in high temperature oven s and kilns. They are programable and will electronically maintain the temperature of the water by cycling the pump and heater. Some can even act as timers. Best practice is to use solid state relays to control the pump and heater separately so an override switch can be utilized to run the pump while soaking and not back feeding other systems. This allows the computer to operate the heating circuits as needed without overheating the hot tub. An analog high limit should be used if the controller doesn't support such features. PID temperature controllers can be as low as $20 on eBay and Amazon. Also available are controllers actually designed for spa use. Single units, programable and dual units that can be set up to control an AC unit to control air temperature as well. A search of "temperature controller thermostat" on eBay or Amazon brings up many small programable units that vary in price but less than $100 can buy a purpose built unit that will handle the basics of running a spa or hut tub. They seem to come with temperature probes and while you may need additional solid state relay circuits to handle the switching of higher loads, these offer promise of being inexpensive solutions that will give some OEM feel to the modern hot tub. Wireless controllers can be had for less than $50 on various sites that will switch loads up to 16 amps and that allow monitoring and control of hot tubs. Your cell phone, computer or other wireless devices are used to control the tub, no normal control panel is available. These are the same controllers people use for automation in the home. Allowing the control lights, heating, etc in their homes. Everything is done over wifi. Sonoff is one of the brands people are having good success with but there are many, many brands to choose from.

5 THERMAL WRAP PUMPS AND LIGHTING

Spa pumps are available with thermal heat wraps. These pumps do away with heaters and are much more efficient in operation. They can also be used WITH existing heaters to allow the best of both worlds. Quick heating and the efficiency gained by utilizing the waste heat of the motor. To maintain the heat day to day when the hot tub isn't occupied. Just control the high power heating element with a switch on relay switching current. Turn it on when you get into the hot tub and off when you get out. Best of both worlds. Maintains temperature well and will better keep up with temperature losses when the top is open. The ones sold today use a snap on hollow plastic housing with passages for water to circulate and soak up heat from the operation of the motor. 120VAC and 240VAC units are available and prices seem to vary between $350 and $400 each. Earlier designs used copper tubing wrapped around the motor. Obviously, this is something anyone could do themselves to an existing pump to save money. The pumps used for this design have an extra outlet and inlet sized appropriately for the hose size needed for the heat jacket, 3/8" if I remember correctly. They usually come in 1 or 1.5 horsepower size. If your application needs more than that to satisfy pressure and flow requirements, two pumps could be used and "T" or "Y" connections used to link them in the flow circuit. These systems do take longer to heat the tub and lose heat more quickly when the top is open but they operate more efficiently and cost less to run. Since they produce less heat, proper insulation of the tub and all parts is an absolute must. Newer hot tub and spa lighting is done with a low voltage two wire system. The lights are LED and are multi color switched by the duty cycle of a square wave signal. They are called RGB LED's. The power supply and control unit isn't inexpensive for these style lamps but some are directly controlled by the spa control board itself. If the board is bad? Retrofitting a single color lamp is the least expensive way to utilize the existing lighting fixture and wiring. I have no idea at all how these multi color lamps would respond to straight DC in either polarity or to low voltage AC. Never had occasion to test it. But, strip lights, are available in indoor, outdoor and marine use and separate controllers are available that may or may not be compatible with your tubs wiring. Multiple wires leaving the controller generally means that the controller unit directly controls the five lead LED bulb where a two wire lead indicates that the logic function happen at the bulb unit, basically half of the circuit exists at the bulb unit. These controllers are very inexpensive and a mistake in purchase means another investment may have to be made in a compatible bulb type that you can retrofit into your tub. Now, all that being said, my little ole' tub has one light. If you feed it 12VDC as I did mine, from a wall transformer using a toggle switch to turn on and off the light, it works just fine. The RBG LED light slowly goes through all its colors and has a very pleasant effect.

So, the conclusion to this in no way complete treatise on low buck hot tub repair is about right here in this last paragraph. I make no claims to any of this being proper or safe. Any information presented here is used at your own risk. Part numbers for your two main analog controls. From hottubspasource.com, H473351080 is your 1/4 inch bulb by 12 inch length high limit thermostat. H473351057 is their corresponding temperature control thermostat. Go through their products to find exactly what you need if these don't suit your needs. Or, try another company. The switches are less than $40 each delivered from most sources, even Amazon has them. Invensys is the brand name of the most commonly available thermostatic switch. A search on Google or another search engine, eBay or Amazon will show you all shapes and sizes of controls and then you can just pick out the best choice by features and price. Once you see the thermostat and part number that you want on a hot tub site, you can search eBay and other places for those part numbers. I have found new old stock parts for pennies on the dollar of regular price.

6 PELLET STOVES AND SMOKERS

Pellet stoves and smokers that use pellets are handy devises but when things go wrong, they can become uneconomical to repair very quickly because of the computers that most use now. Any pellet device that uses an auger to dispense pellets uses a motor that is controlled by a timer or a variable frequency drive. Because these are such low torque motors, full voltage is required to get the torque out of them to do the job of running the auger. So, to control the speed, the frequency of the motor is lowered to slow the rotational speed or a timer is used to pulse the motor to deliver the proper amount of pellets. How do you use a "broken" pellet stove? This portion of the booklet will address what you can do to keep the heat flowing out of a pellet stove when the computer control circuits are fried or become unreliable. There are a few ways we can do this and they vary in expense, difficulty, reliability and safety. Some are improvised work arounds and others are complete replacements of one form of technology for another, while maintaining the use of all the safety gadgets engineered into the appliance. First: Switches and a rheostat to control critical functions. Second: Conversion of stove to burn construction waste of finely cut and split cord wood. Third: Rewiring and installing timers, switches and sensors to make stove function perfectly and safely.

7 SWITCHES AND RHEOSTAT CONTROLS

My first failed stove was old when I got it. I had wanted a pellet stove since they came out but couldn't see the expense of buying one new. I also had a bit of trouble with the idea of being dependent on the supply of a product that I had no control over. What happens if pellets aren't available due to some force beyond my control? I would have a heating appliance that couldn't be adapted to another fuel source? Our favorite gun dealer and long time personal friend in Tonopah had replaced his old one that had warmed us so well in the gun store portion of his house for so many years and while he had intended to take it to the dump, he hadn't found anyone to haul it as yet and after six months on the porch of his gun store, I asked him about it. He told us what the issue was and that he couldn't get it fixed due to parts availability and if we could just haul it away for him, he would be happy. We hauled it and I had it working within a week. It was controlled by timers, switches and a rheostat. It also had a lamp for "power on" and another to tell you when all was well with it's primitive logic system. It provided heat for us for many years and even though we no longer use it, I refuse to get rid of it. The next stove was a bigger one and it was computerized rather than just controlled by timers and a rheostat. Same person gave us that one too, it had belonged to his grown daughter. The control system only worked intermittently and soon after I got the stove, it quit altogether. It was free but I expected more from it and by God I was going to get more. This stove was always used in my shop so I decided to not worry so much about the safety devises and just work on getting it functional and producing heat again. So, as I was laid off from the mine again as funding ran down between investors, money was an object. Quite an object. So, what would it take to get this boat anchor functional on the cheap? A switch to control the exhaust fan, another to control the room fan and something to get some kind of control over the auger motor. All my poor ass self could afford at the time was not much at all. I used a three gang plastic switch box, like those used in residential construction, two light switches and a dimmer switch of the SCR type as I remember. I controlled the fan motors and auger motor separately and without any of the safety snap disk interrupters in circuit. I figured that I could add those later if it worked. I never added them and it has worked for me. The dimmer switch only gives limited speed control as the motor has to have enough torque to sheer pellets and this required quite a bit of voltage. So, somewhat limited control. I was able to use a sheet metal cover on the inside of the bin to restrict pellet entry. That helped greatly and the use of Douglas Fir pellets made quite a bit of difference as well. When this thing was running, it produced so much heat that it would scald you if you got too close to the vents in the front. A bag of pellets only lasted about 8 hours or so until I restricted the pellet feed slot at the auger, inside the bin. The pine pellets would over feed without the restriction plate. They burn a lot slower. With pine pellets at high elevation, restriction of their entry is a must, at least with that stove. At lower elevation, when I used to stove at my shop at work, it functioned much better. I never realized that elevation then resultant difference in O_2 concentration could make such a large difference. Another low buck high torque motor drive that I saw someone use was a corded drill motor, chucked right to the auger and converted to run whenever there was power, the switch was removed and it was wired direct. It was controlled by a rheostat controller from Harbor Freight. You could also take apart your motor and gear box so you could chuck to the gear box, utilizing the supplied gears, assuming that they haven't failed. It would give you more control over speed, which wouldn't be a bad thing if you were going to run the auger continuously vs pulsing it with a timer. It was necessary to modify the tool as delivered though. The controller only gives a certain amount of control as designed and adjusted at the factory. But, what do you expect for $20? More? Read on. The design has an (SCR?) motor drive that is controlled by two rheostats. Two variable resistance potentiometers. The term we used in the industry was "pot". Short for potentiometer. So, that device has two of them. Pot one and pot two. Pot one is for gross adjustment and pot two for minor adjustment. Large vs fine, if you will. The gross adjustment is inside and set at the factory, the minor, or fine adjustment is the knob you see on the face of the unit. This does not give you enough adjustability and pot one isn't easily accessible. Not without modifications. Well, lets get to the modifications. Unplug it.

Take the fuse out of it. Maybe even put a plug lock over it if you want to be ultra safe and make sure noby, including YOU accidently plugs it in while working on it. Now, the back of the unit is glued on at the factory and no service is possible from that point on. So they think. Take the knob off. it is like most pot knobs, it just pulls off. Next, take off the nut holding pot two in place. Next, peel the face sticker off and set it aside so it can be reused. If the glue on this "faceplate" isn't good enough to go back on, contact cement or silicone will serve. Spray adhesive will also work. Once you have access to the panel underneath the faceplate, at approximately the 2:00 position and about 1inch out from the center line of pot 2, drill a 1/2 inch hole in the plastic of the face. I would use a drill press and a Forstner bit. Use your depth control and vise so drilling too deep just can not happen. Look inside and you should see pot one. If it's where it is supposed to be, if not, look for it and cut another access hole once you know where it needs to be. Exploratory surgery is what you are doing if this isn't the same as the one Harbor sells or they have changed it, moving the location of pot one. Once you know where it is on the circuit board below, stick a small screw diver into it so you can plot it's exact location to transfer to the face plate, either with a paper template or by measuring. Drill or punch the hole needed in your faceplate and reassemble the unit. Put the controller in a location suitable for controlling pellet feed and other operational controls of the pellet stove. Wire it into the harness so safety controls are utilized or bypassed if that what you want to do. That is entirely up to you. In use, you would adjust pot one to give pot two enough adjustment for normal appliance operation from low output to high. This would also be a good adaptation for power control of lathe and milling machine table feeds......

8 BURNING CORDWOOD OR CONSTRUCTION WASTE

I was building a lot of outdoor furniture and had quite a pile of 2X4 and 2X6 ends as well as wood too warped to use for furniture. I also had accumulated a lot of demolition wood that wasn't suitable for reuse. It was good enough to burn for heating fuel. I found that the pellet stove would run on it just fine. It tended to smoke a good deal more and soot up the inside and the pipe in a couple days as well as making a lot more ash, but it worked. I just turned off the pellets with a toggle switch and used the other wood and occasionally I also used cord wood cut short and split small. You have to babysit it and feed it every half hour or so but it would run fine and crank out the heat. A few buckets full would run it all day. Seemed much more efficient than a regular wood stove. If you want to use it this way ONLY, just leave the dimmer switch out of the equation and empty your pellet bin, or you can go back and forth between fuel types by adding a toggle switch to interrupt pellet feed like I did. You can also cut a grate out of steel plate, slotting it for the ash to drop through and run it on coal. It was far from perfect but a mixture of coal and wood worked well for me when I tried it, and run time between loadings was extended quite a bit.

9 TIMER CONTROLS

The ultimate conversion does cost more but it puts absolutely reliable control parts in your stove and maintains a level of safety you can't get from switches, a rheostat motor controller or an SCR dimmer switch. You need two snap disk safety switches. Many stoves will already have those devises and it's just a matter of utilizing them. Many newer stoves use a light sensing circuit and this isn't what you need as it requires more circuitry than you will want to deal with. One snap switch is the high limit and it is usually found on the underside of the pellet bin. It will be a normally closed switch. I assume it's there to detect fire in the bin or the overheating associated with a failure of the room fan. It will be in line to the auger motor wiring. The low limit is also in line with the auger motor wiring and it should be on the exhaust tube close to the exhaust fan, at least it was on the one I checked. The idea here is to detect the fire going out and stopping the pellet feed before it completely fills the inside of the fire box. This one should be normally open. Two types of timers are used in the typical installation. One timer is used in conjunction a rheostat to adjust the timer off time and the other one is a 300 second timer activated by a momentary switch to give time for the pellets to start burning properly. This bypasses the normally open snap disk switch on the exhaust tube to give it time to sense the heat of combustion and close, enabling power to reach the pellet feed timer independent of the 900 second timer. You absolutely have to have the first timer and rheostat and the second timer is a safety devise to keep from burying the fire box in pellets if the fire goes out. An "on" lamp is also a nice touch. These parts are also used in older pellet smokers and can be used to resurrect one with a fried computer. A pellet stove supply or an internet search can find you the parts you need and a search can also find you the schematics used by older pellet stoves. A vacuum or pressure switch may be there to control the system in case of exhaust fan circuit or motor failure.

10 PLUGGED AUGER TUBES

This problem can render a pellet stove unfixable in many technicians eyes. Once pellets are exposed to moisture and foul the auger tube by expanding and seizing it tightly? Add rust and then you have an even bigger issue. It's so hard to clean out and the disassembly is so damaging to the auger and drive parts that most appliance technicians just refuse to work on them, calling it a total loss. Well, poor people have poor ways. I already had $25 invested in fixing mine and I wasn't going to loose that money over something some "professional" said couldn't be fixed. I took the pellet auger motor off and used vice grip pliers to try to move the auger at the shaft coupling. It was totally stuck, not even a wiggle. The technician told me it would be. Once I understood how bad things really were because of the expanded pellets and rust, I figured out a plan. I possibly could have used a trickle of water to soften things up but since everything was dry again, I wanted to keep it that way. I drilled into the auger tube from the top with three roughly equally spaced 3/8" holes and used my air compressor, a 1/4" steel tube attached to an air blow gun to start digging away at the blockage, using a small screw driver and curved tools to help loosen the packed wood fibers. Don't do this chore in the house, it throws sawdust everywhere! Safety glasses are a must. After I had worked as much out as I could, I found that the shaft was starting to come loose. I kept wiggling and blowing out more loosened material and soon it would rotate farther and farther. Once it was clear and rotated easily, I reattached to motor, jumped the wiring to allow the motor to run continuously and used a coffee can full of new pellets to clean out the tube. I caught them at the firebox end and sent them through a few times until I was satisfied that the tube was clear enough to function correctly. I put Gorilla Tape over the holes that I had drilled and took the jumper out of my wiring, reattaching to the timer. I used that stove for over two years in our old single wide with 2X4 walls and even though the coldest times of the year at 7000 foot elevation in the high desert frequently dropped below zero on the Fahrenheit scale, that stove and a couple fans dropped our propane cost for heating to practically zero. As remote as we were, using too much propane meant you would run out because the truck couldn't get there in heavy snows and their supply line was stretched pretty thin year 'round. Pellets I could get in town by the bag or by the ton.....

11 PELLET STOVE TIMERS AND PARTS

Infitec Timers are the most common. I wanted to show pictures and links to the company but at time of publishing, they hadn't responded to requests to use their art work.

You need two timers. The first one is a 900 second timer, part number HSS5A1900 and the cost is about $70- $80 depending on your source. Or far more if bought from a stove manufacturer. Sometimes double what it can be bought off eBay. This is a fifteen minute timer that allows the fire to be started and gives time for the low limit snap switch to sense heat and then bypass this timer. If you have trouble getting things going, simply push the start button again before the timer runs down.

The second timer is TRS51A11S2. This timer is one second on time, .3-10 second delay and will work with most stoves. Both of these timers use 120VAC, 230VAC timers are also available. This is the one for small to medium size stoves. Larger stoves or corn stove use a timer with a longer run time. part number TRS51A13S2A give you a three second on time.

A 1 meg ohm potentiometer is required to control this externally adjustable timer. The spec sheet calls for 1/4 watt but the ones I have taken out, replaced and or repaired have always been 2 watt with a metal can casing rather than the plastic fantastic kind. I won't give you any part numbers because parts have been out of stock for the OEM application for many years. These stoves date back to the 90's and later ones using these same timers seem to all have their potentiometers on a control board. The potentiometer will have three terminals, you will use the center and one outside terminal to wire in your remote adjustment for pellet feed.

Other Switches And Parts

Some of the older stoves used a vacuum or pressure switch on the suction side of the exhaust fan. It's contacts will be inline with all other safety devices, should you choose to use it or one like it. Like I mentioned earlier, two snap disk switches were also used for high and low limit, should you want to operate just as safely as possible. The room fan motors in many stoves will be single speed and the switch will control the speeds with a set of fixed resistance values in the switch assembly. They are available but the motor will run just fine on 120 as a single speed if that is more to your needs. There will be an on-off switch. It should be at least a ten amp capacity switch. An on lamp or lighted on-off switch helps you diagnose issues and know when it's on or off. A momentary switch to start the 15 minute or 900 second timer is also required. A lamp to monitor power to your timer circuits is also a plus and this allows you to know when all systems are working properly together. Now, in a pinch, you can figure out what parts are an absolute must and make your own decisions with regards to safety. Most of these stoves will operate on from three to six amps of 120VAC. This makes them ideal candidates for off grid use. You can easily build an inverter right into the cabinet and stub out the proper wiring for DC operation to be hooked into your battery bank or to be ran as a battery backup in the event of a power failure. It can be wired to a UPS as a backup that will allow you to cut pellet feed and shut down safely in the event of a mains failure. If you are on grid, just don't wire it in such a way that back feed of 120 into your house wiring can happen, just for a safety feature.

12 DISCLAIMER

I present no safety, environmental or legal advice in this guide. YOU are responsible to check that any repairs that may be subject to local, state or federal statutes or regulations, are performed to those specifications. I make no claims that anything presented here is safe or suitable for anything at all. This book is published for informational purposes only. Improperly repaired appliances can injure, kill, maim or cause property damage. Repairs or modifications that are made to anything discussed in this book are done so AT YOUR OWN RISK.

As the Navajo say

HOZHO

Walk in beauty my friends......

ABOUT THE AUTHOR

Oh boy, I get to write about myself in the third person? How cool is that?

Tim Johnson has worked in agriculture, aquaculture, logging, milling, mining, and automotive, heavy equipment and truck repair facilities. He has worked as an electrician with electromotive haulage equipment and has also worked in various research and quantitive testing laboratory settings.

Sure sounds like a fart smeller to me......

Made in United States
Troutdale, OR
09/18/2023